THE LITTLE GUIDE TO

GUINNESS

First published in 2026 by OH

An Imprint of HEADLINE PUBLISHING GROUP LIMITED

1

Disclaimer:
This book has not been licensed, approved, sponsored, or endorsed by Guinness or any rightsholder(s) in respect of this brand.

Guinness is a registered trademark owned by Diageo Great Britain Limited

Cataloguing in Publication Data is available from the British Library

ISBN 978-1-03543-339-1

Compiled and written by Malcolm Croft
Editorial: Phoebe Hills
Designed and typeset in Klein Text by Tony Seddon
Project manager: Russell Porter
Production: Marion Storz
Printed and bound in Dubai

Headline's policy is to use papers that are natural, renewable and recyclable products and made from wood grown in well-managed forests and other controlled sources. The logging and manufacturing processes are expected to conform to the environmental regulations of the country of origin.

HEADLINE PUBLISHING GROUP LIMITED
An Hachette UK Company
Carmelite House, 50 Victoria Embankment, London EC4Y 0DZ

The authorised representative in the EEA is Hachette Ireland, 8 Castlecourt Centre, Dublin 15, D15 XTP3, Ireland (email: info@hbgi.ie)

www.headline.co.uk www.hachette.co.uk

THE LITTLE GUIDE TO

GUINNESS

PURE UNOFFICIAL GENIUS

CONTENTS

INTRODUCTION

Arthur Guinness, founder and father of the Guinness brewery in 1759, is the real patron saint of Ireland. Sorry, Patrick, but it's the truth. His legendary ruby red stout porter, with its indulgent creamy head, smooth, velvety mouthfeel, dark roasted notes, and beautiful bitterness – *I'm salivating as I type this!* – is perhaps the biggest, boldest and most beloved "beer" brand in the world, garnering a fierce loyalty and passion from its followers much greater than your average ales. (Let's be honest, no one in their right mind feels as passionately about a pint of Carling lager as Guinness lovers do about their stout.)

In the 21st century, indeed, in just the last five years, Guinness has found itself an entirely new fanbase – Millennials and Generation Z – creating a new boom around this once so-called "old man drink". This renaissance among a younger demographic, aided by social media "Guinnfluencers" yearning for authenticity in an increasingly insincere world, has turned the iconic porter into an iconic trend without it needing to to compromise its history, values or identity. But then, Guinness has always been true to itself and was alreadut a pioneer, a game-changer, constantly pushing the boundaries of technology and innovation. (At first, the company refused to advertise – a revolution in itself – but when it finally did, it was, well, pure genius.)

This *Little Guide to Guinness* is your perfect pub companion. A tiny tome packed with all the facts, stats, wit and wisdom a Guinness connoisseur deserves (and much less expensive than the *Guinness Book of Records*!) This book is a timely, well-deserved celebration of this famous stout – with over 250 years of drinking enjoyment, there's no doubt that the next 250 years of Guinness will be just as exciting, innovative and delicious as the first. And we can't wait. Even though we know good things will come if we do. So, let's raise a toast to the world's favourite porter and remember, *great* things come to those who enjoy Guinness.

Sláinte!

CHAPTER 1

UNCLE ARTHUR

Imagine swimming in a
pool of Guinness – how amazing
would that be?

Anyway, where was I?

Oh yes, it's time to dive into the
thick, creamy world of
Guinness-based wit and wisdom.

Glasses at the ready,
and let's go...

The Real Saint of Ireland

Born in 1725, Arthur Guinness is still today regarded as the "fifth ingredient" of Guinness, alongside water, hops, barley and yeast. A philanthropic man, Arthur established charities, built housing and set up trust funds for Ireland's most vulnerable.

For this, he was affectionately nicknamed "Uncle Arthur" by Dubliners, a name that now extends to his stout. Ask for a pint of "Uncle Arthur" anywhere in Dublin and you'll get a treat.

31 December 1759

The day that Arthur Guinness signed a 9,000-year lease on the four-acre St. James's Gate Brewery in Dublin at £45 a year, approximately worth £11,000 in today's money.

By the mid 1850s, when St. James's Gate had become the largest brewery in the world, Guinness finally bought up all the land and expanded the brewery to cover more than 65 acres.

10 million

The number of glasses of Guinness, on average, consumed worldwide *every day*.

Have you had your pint today?

For 170 years, Guinness refused to advertise and relied solely on word-of-mouth. In 1929, Chairman Rupert Guinness eventually agreed to advertise on one condition: the quality of the advertisements equalled that of the porter.

This mandate initiated a century of creative campaigns, beginning with their first official advertisement in the UK's *Daily Chronicle* in 28 January 1929, famously declaring...

“

Guinness is Good For You

”

Arthur Guinness was initially a successful ale brewer, but after the burgeoning popularity of porter – a dark, rich beer enjoyed by working-class train porters in London in the 1770s – Guinness decided to shift the company's brewing focus.

By 1799, Guinness had ceased making ale and concentrated solely on producing porter.

They've made it every day since.

1.8 billion

The number of pints of Guinness consumed worldwide annually.

“

Make all you can.
Save all you can.
Give all you can.

”

ARTHUR GUINNESS

His personal philosophy to life (and, presumably, Guinness). He adopted this phrase from John Wesley, the founder of Methodism.

Guinness's famous dark ruby red colour comes from **melanoidins**, natural compounds formed during the malting process which convert starches into fermentable sugars.

During this phase, the barley's natural sugars and proteins undergo the **Maillard Reaction** (the same process that browns toast or sears a steak!), a chemical change that creates complex, dark-coloured structures, naturally giving Guinness its distinctive black appearance, without the need for artificial colourings.

19 May 1769

The day Guinness was first exported to England, and the first giant leap in its global expansion.

As exports grew quickly, Guinness soon owned its own fleet of ships, known as the "Guinness Ladies", used to transport its stout across the Irish Sea.

On this first vessel, Guinness shipped just six-and-a-half barrels to Great Britain.

1

The Tilt Test

The "Guinness Tilt Test" is a fun way to gauge the quality of your pint, and has been a viral sensation on social media in recent years.

It involves tilting a pint to a 45-degree angle to see if the creamy, dense head holds firm without spilling.

A perfectly poured pint of Guinness, with its thick, nitrogenated head, should be so stable that it refuses to spill even when tilted significantly.

On June 24, 2025, worldwide pop sensation Olivia Rodrigo performed onstage at Marlay Park, Dublin, wearing a hand-made "Guinness is Good 4 U" t-shirt, a reference to both Guinness's original 1929 advertising slogan and her 2021 hit song, "Good 4 U".

After the show, Olivia posted an image of herself gulping a pint at a pub, proving once and for all that Guinness is no longer an "old man's drink".

"If you come in [to a pub] and order Pepsi and we don't have it, we'll give you Coke. There's no real substitute for Guinness."

ANDY MAC MANUS

The Hard Pour

For those enjoying Guinness from a can at home, and too impatient to pour it properly, try this "Hard Pour" alternative technique, sometimes referred to as "the Flip":

1. Open the can, and wait for the unmistakable hiss to stop.

2. Then, quickly flip the can 180 degrees upside down and pour all the liquid vertically into a pint glass.

3. Slowly lift the can up as the Guinness fills the glass.

4. Let the stout settle to achieve its signature creamy head.

1

What sets Guinness apart from all other beers is its unique gas blend: **70% nitrogen** and **30% carbon dioxide**. (Most beers are simply just carbonated).

The introduction of nitrogen creates significantly smaller, denser bubbles that cascade downwards before rising – known as the Waterfall Effect, or Guinness Cascade – forming its signature creamy, longer-lasting head.

This nitrogen infusion also smooths out the beer's texture and lessens its bitterness, contributing to its famously velvety mouthfeel.

In the 1960s, London socialite Tara Browne, an heir to the Guinness fortune, was a close friend of the Beatles and notably introduced Paul McCartney to LSD.

Tragically, in December 1966, Browne died at just 21 when his Lotus Elan crashed into another car in London's South Kensington.

His untimely death profoundly impacted John Lennon, directly inspiring the haunting opening lyrics of the Beatles' iconic song, 'A Day in the Life':

"I read the news today, oh boy,
about a lucky man who made the grade...
he blew his mind out in a car,
he hadn't noticed that the lights had changed."

The iconic Guinness harp logo, registered as a company trademark in 1876, is based on the famous 14th-century "Brian Boru" harp, which can be viewed at Trinity College, Dublin.

Guinness adopted the harp as its trademark in 1862. When the Irish Free State (now Republic of Ireland) was formed in 1922 and wanted to use the harp as its national emblem, they had to turn it in the opposite direction to avoid infringing on Guinness's existing trademark.

The Guinness harp faces right and the Republic of Ireland's official harp faces left.

In 1939, at the outset of World War II, Guinness made an extraordinary promise, motivated by its own employees serving in the conflict: approximately 900,000 British soldiers would each receive a bottle of Guinness on Christmas Day.

To meet this demand, Guinness workers, retirees, and even staff from other Irish breweries, rallied to help brew the colossal quantity of beer. They succeeded and provided a significant boost to wartime morale – if only for one day.

As of July 2025, the average price for a pint of Guinness in the UK is £4.78*. This is a rise of more than eight per cent since 2024.

In 1959, when Guinness first became nitrogenated, a pint of Guinness in the UK would have cost approximately one shilling, or just 5p in today's money.

**The average cost of a pint of Guinness in America is $7.49.*

Guinness is made from water, barley, roasted malt extract, hops and yeast, with each adding its own essential characteristics:

1. WATER:
sourced for its purity from the Wicklow Mountains

2. MALTED BARLEY:
provides fermentable sugars that the yeast converts into alcohol

3. ROASTED BARLEY:
provides the dark colour and roasty flavour

4. HOPS:
contributes bitterness to balance the sweetness of the malt and acts as a natural preservative

5. YEAST:
the crucial ingredient for fermentation, converting sugars into alcohol

1

17 December 1997

The day Guinness merged with Grand Metropolitan to form Diageo PLC, one of the world's largest multinational beverage companies and today worth more than $55 billion.

Diageo's portfolio contains more than 200 brands, including Johnnie Walker whisky, Smirnoff vodka, Baileys liqueur, Captain Morgan rum, and Tanqueray and Gordon's gins.

Guinness accounts for approximately 16 percent of Diageo's annual sales.

"Guinness –
the wine of Ireland."

JAMES JOYCE

If you're wondering what gives Guinness its bewitching bitter taste, look no further than iso-alpha-acids.

These crucial compounds are naturally present in hops, one of Guinness's four key ingredients.

Extracted during the brewing process, these acids are primarily responsible for imparting a bitterness, a critical component of Guinness's distinctive flavour profile.

1988

The year the first Guinness was enjoyed at home via a can.

While punters were originally unsure of this new product, criticising it as a poor substitution for a pint in a pub, it wouldn't be long before it accounted for one-fifth of all Guinness sales.

13 million

The number of pints of Guinness consumed worldwide on St Patrick's Day – March 17th.

The Guinness Family Curse

The Guinness family has a history as rich and dark as its stout, with many misfortunes haunting the family in the past 250 years:

11 of Arthur Guinness's 21 children did not survive to adulthood.

WALTER EDWARD GUINNESS, a friend of Winston Churchill, was assassinated in Cairo by a Zionist terrorist group during WWII.

TARA BROWNE died in a high-speed car crash in London, aged just 21.

LADY HENRIETTA GUINNESS*
died in 1978 after falling from an aqueduct in Italy.

NATALYA CITKOWITZ,
the 18-year-old daughter of Lady Caroline Blackwood, died from a heroin overdose in 1978.

JOHN GUINNESS
died in a 500-foot fall on Mount Snowdon, Wales, in 1988.

HONOR ULOTH
died in a swimming pool accident at a family barbecue in 2020.

* Henrietta loathed her family's multi-billion-pound wealth: "If I had been poor, I would have been happy," she once said.

“Is it made from Liffey Water?”

PRINCE PHILIP

In 2016, Prince Philip, accompanied by Queen Elizabeth II, visited the Gravity Bar atop the Guinness Storehouse in Dublin. There, he made this now-infamous quip about the stout's dark colour. Historically, Guinness was indeed brewed with water from Dublin's Grand Canal. However, the brewery has long since transitioned to a considerably cleaner water source: the pristine waters from the Wicklow Mountains.) Both the Queen and Prince Philip infamously refused to take a sip of Guinness when they visited, perhaps for fear of getting a thick, foamy "Guinness Moustache".

House of Guinness

A new eight-part Netflix series, *House of Guinness*, is set to air in 2026, chronicling the fortunes (and misfortunes) of the Guinness family.

Created by Stephen Knight (creator or *Peaky Blinders*), the series will star Louis Partridge, James Norton, and Jack Gleason and will explore the family's 19th-century saga between Dublin and New York, beginning after the 1868 death of Benjamin Guinness, Arthur Guinness's grandson and Ireland's then-wealthiest man.

"The Guinness dynasty is known the world over – wealth, poverty, power, influence, and great tragedy are all intertwined," Knight said announcing the series.

CHAPTER 2

BLACK VELVET

While you wait for your first pour to settle, why not use this time wisely... and learn more about Guinness.

Be warned, this chapter is only for the stout of heart!

Introduced in 2010, the Guinness Gravity pint glass is now the most common Guinness-branded pint glass found in pubs and is the preferred vessel for serving the stout.

It presents a sleeker, slightly taller and slimmer profile compared to the classic tulip glass. Its contoured shape is intended to resemble the Guinness harp logo. The wider top and thin, lengthy walls also allow the perfect head to form better.

> People talk about me as if I am the sole inheritor of the Guinness family fortune and worth masses, but I have hundreds of cousins.

JASMINE GUINNESS*

* Born in 1976, Jasmine Guinness is an Irish designer and fashion model, and a direct descendant of Arthur Guinness. She represents the modern face of the extended Guinness family, and its £1 billion+ fortune.

Since 1929, Guinness has teamed up with many creative agencies to create some truly innovative advertising campaigns and taglines:

"Guinness is Good for You" (1929)

"My Goodness, My Guinness" (1935)

"Guinness for Strength" (1935)

"Lovely Day for a Guinness" (1940)

"Pure Genius" (1988)

"There's No Time Like Guinness Time" (1994)

"Good Things Come To Those Who Wait" (1998)

"Believe" (2004)

"noitulovE" (2005)

"To Arthur!" (2009)

"Made of More" (2012)

> Nitrogen is completely inert, and it's three-quarters of what we breathe.

MICHAEL ASH

Guinness was the first brewery in the world to pressurize its beer with nitrogen. The idea for this nitrogenation was conceived by Michael Ash, a Cambridge mathematician who joined the Guinness team in 1951 – the first non-brewer to be recruited into Guinness. Ash masterminded the concept of using nitrogen after watching Guinness sales slump against carbonated beers and ales. By transitioning from traditional oak casks to pressurized kegs containing a precise gas mix of 70 percent nitrogen with 20 per cent carbon dioxide, Ash solved Guinness's "Draft Problem", as it was known. At Guinness, Ash's revolutionary nitro-keg was dubbed 'the Ash Can'.

Guinness is made using a five-step production ritual:

STEP 1: MILLING & MASHING

Making Guinness starts with malted barley, grown by Irish farmers. The malted barley is crushed, then combined with heated water. This mixture is then mashed to extract the brewing sugars, then dropped into a mash tun to separate the liquid (or "sweet wort") from the grains.

STEP 2: ROASTING

The next stage is what gives Guinness its unique taste and rich ruby colour. The barley is dark-roasted at exactly 232 degrees Celsius. Hops and roasted barley are then added to the sweet wort to balance and enhance the flavour.

STEP 3: BOILING

The sweet wort is boiled for 90 minutes, then left to cool and settle.

STEP 4: FERMENTATION AND MATURATION

The Guinness yeast is added to the sweet wort, then everything is left to mature. The Guinness yeast strain has been passed down from generations.

STEP 5: STORAGE

Since 1959, Guinness has used a mixture of 70 per cent nitrogen and 30 per cent carbon dioxide in its kegs.

$4.6 billion

The global value of the Guinness brand, making it the most valuable and recognizable Irish brand in the world.

In 2025, some financial reports suggest a potential value exceeding $10 billion if Guinness were to be sold.

“

If you could just leave us in peace... until I finish this lovely pint of Guinness.

”

HARRY HART

The idea for the hit film Kingsman: The Secret Service, starring Colin Firth and Taron Egerton, originated in 2014 when director Matthew Vaughn was "pouring back several pints of Guinness" in a pub. There, he conceived a fresh take on the spy genre. To honour this inspiration, a memorable scene features Colin Firth's character, Harry, drinking a pint of Guinness just before he transforms into a formidable fighting machine, with an "A Guinness for strength" advertisement prominently displayed behind him for good measure.

Hops, the female flower of the *Humulus lupulus* plant, are crucial for brewing Guinness. They provide the stout with its famous bitterness, flavour and aroma. In the early 1800s, Guinness brewers relied on hops as a natural preservative to keep their stout fresh on long sea voyages.

Hop plants thrive only in countries that are between the latitudes of 35 and 55 degrees north and south of the equator, including England, the United States, Australia, New Zealand, Germany and the Czech Republic.

300 tonnes

The amount of Irish barley, Guinness receives every week from its 900 barley growers.

Barley, a cereal grain and member of the grass family, was one of the first grains ever cultivated by humans, dating back around 9,000 BC.

The word "beer" originates from the Anglo-Saxon word "baere", meaning barley.

The Six-Step Pour

Pouring a perfect and precise pint of Guinness is an art. This is the "Six-Step Pour" that Britain's biggest pub chain, Wetherspoons*, stands proudly by for each pint:

Step 1
Take a clean, dry, Guinness-branded glass. A Gravity Glass works best.

Step 2
Hold the glass firmly at 45° under the tap. Make sure the tap does not touch the glass.

Step 3
Pull the handle fully forwards, towards you, slowly straightening the glass as it fills, stopping when it is three-quarters full.

Step 4
Leave the surge to settle for two minutes, allowing the creamy head to form.

Step 5
Top up the glass by pushing the tap handle away from you. Stop when the head is proud of the rim.

Step 6
Present the perfect pint to the customer with the Guinness logo facing forwards.

** All 800 Wetherspoon pubs in the UK have achieved Guinness accreditation. This accreditation is an annual assessment by Diageo assessors, involving unannounced visits to purchase and assess the quality of a pint of Guinness. The assessment focuses on the six-step process for pouring a perfect pint, ensuring it is served at the correct temperature, with the proper head, and within the specified time.*

Around eight per cent of the total barley used in a typical Guinness brew is roasted.

This roasting process occurs at precisely 232 degrees Celsius, a temperature critical for developing its unique flavour and colour without burning the grain.

“Guinness 0.0, thank God for it.”

COLIN FARRELL

During the filming of 2022's Oscar-winning *The Banshees of Inisherin*, Irish stars Colin Farrell and Brendon Gleason were allowed to drink Guinness 0.0 repeatedly during takes without getting drunk.

On previous productions, if an actor had to drink Guinness on screen, a prop master would have to concoct a ghastly mixture, usually grape juice with (curdled) cream, or "flat coke with all sorts of unspeakables on top of it," according to Gleason. "It's important to suffer for art, and this was suffering," Gleason said of his experiences with fake movie Guinness.

Not quite a *Guinness World Record*, but close: In 2024, Sean Bryan of Kilkenny, Ireland, gained viral online fame for drinking 81 pints of Guinness across the New Year's Eve weekend.

The session amounted to him consuming 186 alcohol units and more than 17,000 calories – much, *much* more than the recommended amount of either.

“

I’m not obsessive about fitness. I work out three or four times a week but I take the weekends off and drink as much Guinness as I can get down my neck.

”

DANIEL CRAIG

International Stout Day

is observed worldwide on the first Thursday of November every year.

Since its launch in November 2018, Dublin's Guinness Storehouse has been creating picture-perfect pints with its STOUTie machine.

This specialized printer transforms the beer's creamy foam head into a personalized canvas using a harmless, edible ink made from malt extract. The STOUTie can print custom graphics, messages, and even detailed photos directly onto the stout in under 10 seconds.

Unsurprisingly, the most popular choice of art for punters looking to customize their pint is a selfie.

Six degrees Celsius (42.8°F)

The optimum temperature at which to enjoy a pint of Guinness.

At home, to properly chill a can of Guinness, you should refrigerate it for at least 24 hours before opening. This ensures the beer reaches the ideal serving temperature for optimal taste and experience.

In 1991, the “rocket widget” – the small ball at the bottom of all Guinness Draught cans – won the Queen’s Award for Technological Advancement in 1991, and was recognised as one of the greatest invention of the past 40 years.

How it works is a marvel: When the can’s ring pull is opened, the internal pressure drops. This causes the nitrogen-filled widget to release its gas through a tiny hole into the stout, creating millions of tiny bubbles. These nitrogen bubbles guarantee a creamy head and the iconic “Guinness Cascade”.

"Like so many things in life, a well-poured pint of Guinness is worth waiting for."

RASHERS TIERNEY

119.5 seconds

Known as "Guinness time", the precise 119.5-second countdown is the scientifically determined optimal settling period for a Guinness Draught between its two pours.

This wait allows the 300 million tiny, densely packed nitrogen bubbles to complete their journey to the top of the glass, creating a stable, tight and creamy head.

Splitting the G

Among the many enduring Guinness drinking traditions, "Splitting the G" is perhaps the most famous.

The goal of this challenge is to take a single, precise glug of Guinness so that the foamy line of the head falls perfectly halfway between the "G" in the Guinness logo on the glass.

To achieve this, you'll need an accurately timed gulp, usually the equivalent of four standard sips.

Ideally, a pint of Guinness should be consumed in four to five gulps.

To best enjoy a pint of Guinness, it's recommended that large gulps be taken from the glass rather than sipping. This method ensures a proper integration of the creamy head with the stout beneath, rather than just sipping pure head.

This method is authentically Irish and known as the "Guinness way" of drinking stout.

An Irish Toast to Guinness

My dear friends,
they're the best friends,
each is loyal, trust-worthy
and able.

But now it's time for drinking,
so lift all of your glasses
off the table!

> “When I die I want to decompose in a barrel of porter and have it served in all the pubs in Dublin. I wonder would they know it was me?”

J. P. DUNLEAVY

An Irish Toast to Guinness

When we drink,
we get drunk.

When we get drunk,
we fall asleep.

When we fall asleep,
we commit no sin.

When we commit no sin,
we go to heaven.

So, let's all get drunk,
and go to Heaven!

"

I'm an early riser.
I work out really hard.
I push myself; I get my job
done, and at the end of
the day, there's a Guinness
waiting for me.

"

JASON MOMOA

CHAPTER 3

THE SURGE & THE SETTLE

With our perfect pint
patiently waiting
for the surge to occur,
and not wishing to
settle for anything less,
let's pause for a
moment.

Ready to continue?

Let the surge commence!

“

Oh Beer! Oh Hodgson,
Guinness, Allsop, Bass!

Names that should be on
every infant's tongue!

Shall days and months and
years and centuries pass,

And still your merits be
unrecked, unsung?

”

CHARLES STUART CALVERLEY

The only thing better than a pint of Guinness is...

Another pint of Guinness.

Guinness relies on a unique, highly guarded strain of *Saccharomyces cerevisiae* yeast, integral to its distinct taste since the 20th century.

This mighty yeast is the engine of brewing, transforming sweet wort into stout. It not only creates alcohol but also produces specific flavour compounds essential to Guinness's signature taste.

To maintain consistency, a small amount of yeast from each brew is transferred to the next. Master cultures are stored in liquid nitrogen tanks at -196°C, safeguarding the yeast for future brews.

“

What do Dubliners do here better than any other place on earth? Answer: Guinness. This delicious, some say magical, probably nutritious, unparalleled beverage. This divine brew is so tasty, creamy, so near chocolatey in its rich, satisfying, buzz-giving qualities, that the difference between the stuff here, and the indifferently poured swill you get where you come from, is like night and day. One is beer, the other, angels sing celestial trombones.

”

ANTHONY BOURDAIN

300 million

The number of nitrogen and carbon dioxide bubbles, in a 70-30 split respectively, in every pint of Guinness.

“I do like Guinness,
I have to say, because you
feel like you’re
eating something.”

LEWIS BLACK

After four years of development, Guinness 0.0 – the non-alcoholic version of Draught Guinness – was initially launched in October 2020.

However, just one month after its release, Guinness initiated a significant recall of millions of cans due to "microbiological contamination", rendering the stout unsafe for consumption.

Following thorough investigations, Guinness 0.0 successfully relaunched in June 2021 and has since quickly become the UK's biggest-selling alcohol-free beer.

3

17:59 (5:59 p.m.)

The precise time that has become a beloved, unofficial tradition for enjoying your first pint of Guinness. This precise minute playfully celebrates the year 1759, when Arthur Guinness signed the famous 9,000-year lease for the St. James's Gate Brewery in Dublin.

It's also conveniently timed for your first post-work pint, making it the perfect moment to raise a toast to Uncle Arthur.

September 24 - Arthur's Day!

In 2009, Guinness launched "Arthur's Day" to commemorate Arthur Guinness and the 250th anniversary of his brewery.

This global celebration of music and the raising of toasts ran for five years. However, Guinness cancelled the event in 2013 as critics, including public health advocates, argued it had become less about genuine celebration and more a marketing campaign encouraging excessive alcohol consumption.*

*You can still celebrate World Guinness Day on this day, if you prefer...

Is fearrde an Guinness thú

(You are the better for Guinness)

A common Gaelic expression in Ireland

"

We are brewers and always have been; and in our brewing we have sought, and we seek, to ally the traditions and craftsmanship of the past with the best that science has to teach us.

"

RUPERT GUINNESS

3

A standard pint of Guinness Draught contains approximately 210 calories. For decades, Guinness countered the persistent urban legend that it contained as many calories as a full roast dinner. In reality, a pint of Guinness is actually the equivalent to just one slice of pizza, effectively debunking a long-held misconception it was a “meal in a glass”.

A 2011 study in the *Journal of Food Science* found scientific evidence to support the well-known belief that Guinness tastes better in Ireland. Researchers conducted 100 blind tastings across 14 countries, revealing pints in Irish pubs consistently scored significantly higher on enjoyment. While not pinpointing a single cause, the study suggested Guinness "does not travel well." It highlighted factors such as the unique atmosphere of Irish pubs, the cleanliness of high-volume beer lines and expert pouring techniques, as key contributors.

“

This is the best thing that happens to me all night – a pint of cold Guinness.

”

DENIS LAWSON

"

Shaun: As Bertrand Russell once said, 'The only thing that will redeem mankind is cooperation.' I think we can all appreciate the relevance of that now.

Liz: Was that on a beer mat?

Shaun: Yeah, it was Guinness Extra Cold.

"

Shaun of the Dead, 2004,
Written by Edgar Wright and Simon Pegg

In 1997, Guinness launched its now famous "Not Everything in Black and White Makes Sense" beer mat marketing campaign. The campaign aimed to make drinkers re-examine the brand by presenting implausible scenarios accompanied by memorable quotations. Some of the most famous quotes were:

Did 36% of strippers have a convent education?

Do men think about sex every six seconds?

and Vic Reeves' immortal joke:
88.2% of all statistics are made up on the spot.

The campaign significantly contributed to Guinness achieving its highest ever market share in 1998.

"Ba mhaith líom píonta Guínness, le do thoíl"

"I'd like a pint of Guinness, please,"

How to order your pint of Guinness in Gaelic

An Irish Toast to Guinness

Let the winds of fortune sail you,
And may you sail a gentle sea.

And let it always be the
other fella who says,
"Lads – this drink's on me."

To truly sound like a local Dubliner, don't just order a "pint of Guinness", ask for a "pint of gat" instead.

This handy bit of Irish slang is a colloquial term you'll often hear in Dublin pubs, instantly marking you as a true Guinness connoisseur.

In the US, Guinness sales makes up two per cent of the total beer market.

In the UK, Guinness is the most popular draught beer and accounts for 11 per cent of all beer sales.

“The first time I had Guinness is when I came to Shannon airport. We were flying into Afghanistan and so stopped in Shannon. It was the middle of the night. I tried one and I realised it tastes so much better here than it does in the States... You're keeping all the best stuff here!”

BARACK OBAMA

3

While Guinness may be nicknamed “the black stuff”, it’s actually a very dark ruby red.

If you hold a pint up to the light, you can see the deep red hue, which comes from the roasted unmalted barley.

The name “Guinness” comes from an Anglicized form of the Gaelic “Mag Aonghusa” meaning “son of Angus”.

The name Angus is of Irish Gaelic origin and means “one choice” or “one strength”, hence why the brand’s former legendary advertising motto was “Guinness Gives You Strength”.

No pint of Guinness is complete without the iconic Irish toast of Sláinte.

While often mistaken for "cheers", "Sláinte" actually means "Health".

To properly pronounce "Sláinte", it's said as "Slaan-cha".

St. Patrick's Day - 17 March!

This day honours Ireland's patron saint, St. Patrick. What began as a religious feast day in the 17th century has evolved into a global celebration

3

One third of all pints of beer consumed in Ireland are Guinness.*

*Approximately, 300,000 pints are enjoyed in Ireland every single day.

Guinness Playlist

"Hey Porter" – Johnny Cash

"Black or White" – Michael Jackson

"Ruby Tuesday" – Melania Safka

"Guinness Stout" – Any Given Sunday

"Black Velvet" – Alannah Miles

"The Wind That Shakes the Barley" – Irish Folk Song

"Head" – Prince

"Cream" – Prince

"Bubbles Up" – Jimmy Buffett

"Irish Stout" – Brian de Marco

20,000

The number of pints of Guinness the famous central London pub, The Devonshire, sells every single week – by far the biggest-selling single retailer of Guinness anywhere in the world.

"The 20,000 pints of Guinness a week thing is true!" landlord Oisín Rogers said of this astonishing sales feat, though, somewhat ironically, it has yet to be verified by the *Guinness World Records.*

CHAPTER 4

A THICK HEAD

A pint of Guinness
famously has a thick head,
but rarely does it
leave you with one – even
if you enjoy one too many.

Take one last look
at that white creamy
foam-dome,
because we're about to
split that G.

Let's go!

Launched in 2021, the Guinness Nitrosurge is a portable, rechargeable nozzle designed to attach to Nitrosurge cans of Guinness Draught.

When activated, its patented ultrasonic transducer utilizes a specifically tuned wavelength and frequency to precisely break down the nitrogen in the beer, creating the signature Guinness surge.

Two million

The number of pint glasses stolen in the UK every single year, costing pubs more than £186 million per year.

One recent survey has found that 37 million Brits have stolen glasses in their homes.

The most popular pint glass stolen? You've guessed it – Guinness.

“

A stout heart breaks bad luck.

”

MIGUEL DE CERVANTES

“

St. Patrick’s Day
is named for St. Patrick,
the first guy
to feed Guinness
to a snake.

”

CONAN O’BRIEN

1.8 million

The number of international tourists who visit the Guinness Storehouse in Dublin every year, making it far and away Ireland's most popular tourist attraction.

The seven-storey landmark, built in 1904, opened as the Storehouse in 2000, and was the first skyscraper erected in the British Isles.

To date, it has welcomed more than 25 million tourists, including scores of celebrities, including Tom Cruise, Will Ferrell and Kylie Minogue.

A Guinness Joke

Two men are in a bar. One says, "I bet you can't drink a whole pint of Guinness in one go." The other agrees and leaves the bar.

He returns 30 minutes later and downs the Guinness in one. The first man asks, "Why did you leave?"

The other replies, "I went to the pub across the road to practice."

A Toast to Guinness

May your glass be ever full.

May the roof over your head be always strong.

And may you be in Heaven half an hour before the Devil knows you're dead.

4

Nigeria is home to the first-ever overseas Guinness brewery, established in Ikeja, Lagos, in 1962, and today Nigeria stands as the second-largest global market for Guinness behind the UK.

The country primarily enjoys Guinness Foreign Extra Stout, a stronger bolder brew (around 7.5% ABV, compared to the regular 4.2% ABV) and is specifically adapted for local tastes using local ingredients such as maize (corn), instead of barley.

$P = kHC$

When Michael Ash first nitrogenated the Guinness stout using a precise mixture of nitrogen and CO_2, he used **Henry's Law** as his guide. This law states that dissolved gas in a liquid is proportional to the gas's partial pressure above it.

For Guinness, this explains both its carbon dioxide content and, crucially, its nitrogenation. Nitrogen, being far less soluble than CO_2, requires higher pressure to dissolve. When a pint is poured or a can opened, the sudden pressure drop forces these dissolved gases out of solution, creating Guinness's cascading effect and creamy head. Remember that science next time you have a pint!

Guinness is produced using high-gravity brewing in Dublin. This means it's initially brewed to a higher alcoholic strength, typically around 8% ABV.

The concentrated liquid is then transported in tankers, and then diluted with specially treated water once it reaches its final destination, to achieve its final retail strength, usually 4.2% ABV for Draught.

This high gravity method ensures a consistent Guinness flavour globally and optimizes distribution with a lower carbon footprint.

By 1886, St. James's Gate had become the world's largest brewery, expanding from its original four acres (1759) to 65 acres.

At its late-19th-century peak, it functioned as a self-contained city within Dublin, employing more than 5,000 people – the city's largest single employer.

The brewery also boasted its own railway system, a fleet of barges for transport, and housing and welfare service provision for its workforce, making it Ireland's most powerful economic force.

“What we do every St. Patty’s day is wear green and drink a lot of Guinness. And maybe cry a little bit and laugh, and everyone has to sing a song.”

SAOIRSE RONAN

“

In coming to the Guinness Storehouse, Catherine and I are retracing the footsteps of my grandmother (Queen Elizabeth II) who was shown how to pour the perfect pint here in 2011. Ladies and gentlemen, let me tell you it is not often that I find myself following the Queen to a pub. But I am looking forward to testing for myself the theory that Guinness tastes even better in Ireland than overseas.

”

PRINCE WILLIAM

Dublin's Guinness Storehouse features a spectacular seven-story glass atrium designed to resemble a giant pint glass.

If this immense central space were to be filled with Guinness, it would hold a staggering 14.3 million pints – approximately the same amount of pints of Guinness consumed on St Patrick's Day, coincidentally.

A Guinness Joke

An Irish man frees a genie. Happy to be released from his confinement, the genie grants him three wishes.

The Irishman thinks about it, and says, "I want me a pint of Guinness that never goes empty." Magically, a pint appears, filled to the rim with the rich dark drink.

The man drinks it down, and when he places it back on the bar, it fills up again. "AMAZING!" exclaims the Irishman. "So, what would you like for your other two wishes, sir?" asks the genie.

The Irishman, thinking of all the Guinness he'll be drinking says, "I want two more of these, then!"

“

Fanny ate a whole foul for breakfast, to say nothing of a tower of hot cakes. Belle and I floored another hen between the pair of us, and I shall be no sooner done with the present amanuensis racket than I shall put myself outside for a pint of Guinness.

”

ROBERT LOUIS STEVENSON

1893

“

Pint of Guinness, please. No logo on the foam. You don’t buy into all that one, do ya? What, the old, ‘Oo, I’ve got a clover in me foam, I’m so important.’ No, what you’re doing there is you’re drinking an advert, ain’t ya, eh, shithead?

”

SUPER HANS

Peep Show.

“Guinness – the nicest drink ever invented.”

KING CHARLES III

In 1935, Irish artist John Gilroy, from S.H. Benson advertising company, created Guinness's iconic "My Goodness, My Guinness" campaign. Inspired by a circus visit, Gilroy depicted zoo animals humorously interacting with the stout.

The first poster showed a zookeeper chasing a Guinness-stealing sea lion. This led to famous ads featuring ostriches, crocodiles, and notably, Gilroy the Toucan – with its beloved "Lovely day for a Guinness!" slogan – which became a beloved mascot until the 1980s and remains a cherished brand symbol today.

> People come to Ireland looking for the Holy Grail – the perfect pint. People are always looking for that. That's why Guinness is such a legend.

FERGAL MURRAY

Guinness Master Brewer

“

No other beer has to go through a ritual. We make the ritual important. It's theatre. The ceremony behind pouring a pint is essential to the consumer's requirement for a perfect pint of Guinness. It's all part of the indefinable essence. The ritual and the crafting of the pint is about serving the beverage to your customer in the right way. With any other beer, you can just put it under the tap and hand it out. But with Guinness you've got to think about it.

”

FERGAL MURRAY

Guinness Master Brewer

“

Dear Jack, this white mug that
with Guinness I fill,

And drink to the health of sweet
Nan of the Hill,

Was once Tommy Tosspot’s, as jovial a sot

As e’er drew a spigot, or drain’d a full pot—

In drinking all round ‘twas his joy to
surpass,

And with all merry tipplers he swigg’d
off his glass.

”

WILLIAM MAKEPEACE THACKERAY

Durlesques, 1852

Beyond the Guinness Storehouse, Mulligan's pub on Poolbeg Street is Dublin's most famous spot for a perfectly poured pint of Guinness.

Established in 1782, this now legendary pub boasts a long list of famous patrons. Notably, John F. Kennedy, then a young Congressman, and America's first Irish-Catholic president, enjoyed his first ever pint of Irish Guinness here during his first visit to Ireland in 1947.

A Guinness Joke

An Irishman goes into a bar and orders three pints of Guinness. The bartender serves them to him and asks, "Why the three?" The Irishman replies, "One for me, one for me brother who's in America, and one for me brother over in Australia." "Nice.", replies the barman.

This continues for months, the man coming in regularly to order his three pints, until one day the Irishman only orders two pints.

Sure that one of his kin must have passed, the bartender approaches. "Is everyone okay? Is there some bad news?" The Irishman replies," Oh yeah, everyone is fine... I just decided to quit drinking'."

“That first sip is so refreshing, such a robust flavour. The first one’s gone before it even hits the counter. When you get a great pour, there’s a little bit of art to it. Guinness is my drink of choice.”

JOHN CENA

"I love Guinness absolutely 1,000 per cent. It's my favourite beer. I have it in my house in keg form. I actually pour drafts in my house."

PAUL RUDD

“

I had a very good friend who lived in London called Tara Browne, a Guinness heir – a nice Irish guy.

”

PAUL MCCARTNEY

In 1966, McCartney had a now-infamous moped accident with Browne, where he hit the pavement and split his lip. This incident directly led to McCartney growing a moustache, primarily to conceal the stitches on his lip. This marked a significant shift in the Beatles' appearance, as McCartney became the first band member to sport facial hair. By 1967, all the Beatles – and millions of their male fans – adopted the look, sparking a global trend for facial hair. This change in appearance is often seen as symbolic of the band's artistic maturation.

“

I was drinking stout aged five, I used to get two bottles of Guinness a night. If anyone questioned my family about it they would say, ‘If you give him enough when they’re young, they won’t go overboard with it later on’. You soon get used to two bottles of Guinness a night.

”

SHANE MACGOWAN

CHAPTER 5

IRELAND'S WINE

From the first sip to
the last, Guinness tickles
the spots most other
beers cannot reach.

That moment of
happiness after that
first gulp massages
the back of your throat
is the taste of home.

It's little wonder
the Irish are so proud to
call it their own...

"

Put cream cheese on a Guinness – and I'm there. You've not lived until you've eaten a Guinness cake.

"

BLAKE LIKELY

The water used for Guinness at St. James's Gate Brewery originates from the Poulaphouca Reservoir in County Wicklow, collected from the Wicklow Mountains, approximately 40km away.

This exceptionally soft water type is characterized by its low mineral content, ideal for brewing Guinness.

While some believe it contributes to Guinness tasting better in Dublin, it's the water's specific composition – allowing the rich malt flavours to shine without mineral interference – that's crucial.

Black Velvet

The legendary Black Velvet cocktail was created in 1861 at Brook's Club, London, to mourn the death of Queen Victoria's husband, Prince Albert.

This mix of equal parts Guinness and champagne was designed to symbolize the black armbands worn by mourners.

The recipe is simple yet delicious: half fill a Champagne flute with Guinness, then slowly top it up with chilled Champagne. Talk about effervescence.

5

Irish literary giant James Joyce dabbled in Guinness slogans in his notoriously complex 1939 novel *Finnegans Wake*.

He famously suggested "Guinness – The Free, The Flow, the Frothy Freshener!" as an alternative to "Guinness is Good for You", the then-famous Guinness slogan.

In 1901, Guinness opened its Experimental Brewery, a scientific research laboratory at its St. James's Gate Brewery, the very first of its kind.

There, in 1907, William Sealy Gosset developed a groundbreaking statistical tool known as the Student's t-test. It was initially used as quality control in small batches of brewing ingredients such as barley, but soon became a cornerstone of modern statistics.

Its applications now span countless scientific fields, from medicine to agriculture, and was a profound contribution to the world of data analysis.

Opened in 2014 at Dublin's St. James's Gate, Brewhouse 4 is Guinness's state-of-the-art brewing facility.

At a cost of £169 million, it stands as the most environmentally sustainable and technologically advanced brewery globally and the first major brewery to be awarded the highest certifications in eco-sustainability.

Most importantly, it's capable of producing 2,000 pints of Guinness every hour!

2.2 million

The number, on average, of Guinness pints consumed in the UK every single day, making it Britain's No.1 most sold "beer" in pubs.

5

An Irish Toast to Guinness

May the luck of the Irish
Lead to happiest heights
And the highway you travel
Be lined with green lights.

Wherever you go and
whatever you do,

May the luck of the Irish
be there with you.

Purple Guinness

A well-known, if typically British pub creation in the UK, Purple Guinness offers a simple yet tasty twist on a pint of plain.

To make it, simply add 30ml (approximately two tablespoons) of Ribena or any blackcurrant cordial to your pint glass, then slowly top it up with Guinness.

The cordial introduces a fruity sweetness that cuts through the stout's bitterness, transforming the beer's deep ruby-red hue into a bright purple.

5

The Toucan

Among London's most celebrated Guinness pubs is The Toucan, located at 19 Carlisle Street, Soho. Named after John Gilroy's advertising toucan, the pub's legendary passion for Guinness has cemented its reputation as the city's perfect spot for a perfect pint.

Patrons often descend to its famous Guinness-themed basement bar, a dedicated space bursting with decades-old Guinness memorabilia. In recent years, the pub has become a pilgrimage for the Guinness connoisseur and, during the 1960s, was a beloved haunt of Guinness drinker, Jimi Hendrix.

August 27, 1955

The day the very first edition of *The Guinness Book of Records* was published. In 1951, the then-managing director of Guinness, Sir Hugh Beaver, had the idea for the book while attending a shooting party in County Wexford, Ireland. The group debated which was the fastest game bird in Europe, and after finding no reference book to settle the argument, he realized the potential for a trivia book that could resolve simple pub disputes.

When, in 1954, Sir Hugh had the idea for a Guinness promotion based on the idea of settling pub arguments he asked Norris and Ross McWhirter, two fact-finding researchers from Fleet Street, to compile a book of facts and figures. To date, the book has sold more than 150 million copies across 100 countries as it is updated every year.

5

In Malaysia, and many other parts of Asia, if you order a “Black Dog”, you’ll almost certainly be handed a cold bottle of Guinness Foreign Extra Stout, the drink that accounts for almost half of Guinness sales worldwide.

"

A bird never flew on one wing.

"

Irish proverb: you can't have just one Guinness.

5

Designed to look like the head of a pint of Guinness towering above the famous St. James's Gate Brewery, and located 46 metres off the ground, the Guinness Storehouse's seventh-story Gravity Bar is the highest bar in Dublin.

On a clear day, punters can see the expansive mountain range, the Wicklow Mountains in the background, where Guinness sources all of its pristine water for brewing and St. Patrick's Cathedral in the foreground, the ancient site of worship of Ireland's most famous saint.

"A man takes a drink; the drink takes a drink; the drink takes the man."

Irish Proverb

"

It's Saint Patrick's day. Here in Scranton, St. Patty's day is a big deal. It is the closest the Irish will ever have to Christmas.

"

MICHAEL SCOTT

The Office

One in every nine pints sold annually in London is a Guinness.

*Londoners drink 1.4 billion pints every year.

“There can be nothing more frequent than an occasional drink.”

OSCAR WILDE

Oscar Wilde, the famous Irish writer, was even more famed for his love of drink. There's even a Guinness-based cocktail named after him, the 'Wilde Oscar' presumably something he drank to make him even wittier. To make it, simply add 37.5ml of Irish Whiskey to 25ml of Guinness, along with 12.5ml of Sugar Syrup and two dashes of Angostura Bitters to a glass filled with ice cubes. Stir, then garnish with orange zest and a Maraschino Cherry.

A Guinness Joke

Two Irishmen are lost at sea and find a bottle. One of them uncorks it and a genie comes out.

"I shall grant you one wish for freeing me," says the genie.

"I wish the whole ocean were made of Guinness!" blurts out the first Irishman.

"Done!" exclaims the genie, and with a nod of his head, the water turns to the black stout as far as the eye can see.

"You idiot!" screams the second Irishman. "Now we'll have to piss in the boat!"

Guinness pairs well with food, particularly with hearty dishes such as stews, meat pies, chocolate desserts and, even, oysters.

At Dublin's iconic Temple Bar, one of its legendary offerings is the "Oysters and Guinness Experience": 12 fresh Galway Bay oysters (the home of Irish oysters) and a pint of Guinness. The stout's creamy, roasted notes perfectly complement the salty oysters.

Not to be missed.

"Ireland sober is Ireland stiff."

JAMES JOYCE

5

3.5 million

The total number of pints Guinness produces every single day at St. James's Gate Brewery, making it the biggest stout export brewery on the planet.

400

The total number of quality control checks carried out on every brew at St. James's Gate Brewery, scrutinizing every stage from raw ingredients to the finished stout.

A dedicated team of experts, dubbed "super tasters", also conduct 23 taste tests before any keg leaves the brewery.

This commitment to quality ensures the consistent flavour, colour and texture of every pint, and is an example of Guinness's scientific approach to brewing since the establishment of its laboratory in 1901

5

Today, Guinness no longer exclusively serves just stout porter – it now offers more than 20 drinkable products.

Since 2015, the brand has expanded into lager too, firstly with its Hop House 13, primarily brewed in Dublin, as well as the Guinness Baltimore Blonde, made at the Open Gate Brewery in Baltimore, USA for the American market. It's a lighter, crisp blonde lager at around 5% ABV.

"

He waits. That's what he does.

And I'll tell you what. Tick followed tock followed tick followed tock, followed tick.

Ahab says, 'I don't care who you are, here's to your dream.'

The old sailors returned to the bar. 'Here's to you, Ahab!'

And the fat drummer hits the beat with all his heart.

Here's to waiting.

"

"Surfer'" Ad, 1999. Read by Louis Mellis

In 2000, Guinness's 1999 "Surfer" advert was named the best TV commercial of all time in a UK poll.

Directed by Jonathan Glazer, this iconic monochromatic ad drew inspiration from Melville's *Moby Dick* and Walter Crane's "Neptune's Horses". It powerfully depicted Polynesian surfers riding massive, slow-motion waves alongside galloping horses, set to Leftfield's heavy-beat "Phat Planet".

The ad masterfully symbolized the patience required for a perfect Guinness pour, while also transforming perceptions that Guinness was an "old man's drink".

Guinness Martini

One of the most ordered cocktails in the world, the Guinness Martini gets every party started.

Pour 50ml of dark rum into a jug with a handful of ice and add 25ml cold espresso coffee, 25ml vodka, 25ml crème de cacao and 100ml Guinness.

Stir with a spoon until the outside of the jug feels cold then strain into two martini glasses and serve.

Enjoy – responsibly!

Since it first flung open its doors in 1759, Guinness was a pioneering employer,* offering staff two pints of Guinness a day for every male employee over the age of 21, in addition to their salaries, of course.

In the 1960s, Guinness reduced these free entitlements down to two bottles. Today, all Guinness employees are given a €50 monthly credit for the Diageo online shop to spend as they wish.

*In addition to free stout, Guinness also typically pays its workers up to 20 per cent more than the Dublin average.

CHAPTER 6

SLÁINTE & TÁINTE

As we approach our final gulp, it's time to let that perfectly poured pint of Guinness sink in.

There's no greater feeling.

Here's to your health and your wealth. Here's to waiting.

Here's to your dream.

A persistent 19th-century urban legend about St James's Gate Brewery is that a rats were once discovered inside the vats during cleaning.

The myth recounts that after thorough sterilisation, the next brew lacked a taste Guinness drinkers had grown to appreciate.

Soon, speculation arose that the dead rats inadvertently contributed a unique flavour profile to the stout!

TODAY, NO RATS ARE USED IN THE MAKING OF GUINNESS.

6

In 2017, Guinness became fully suitable for vegans after it altered its traditional filtration process to eliminate isinglass, a byproduct derived from dried fish bladders.

Historically, isinglass has been used as a fining agent in brewing to clarify beer by binding to yeast and other particles, causing them to settle.

TODAY, NO DRIED FISH BLADDERS ARE USED IN THE MAKING OF GUINNESS.

Film star Rutger Hauer's legendary "Pure Genius" campaign for Guinness ran from 1987 to 1994, and profoundly transformed the brand's global reputation.

Hauer, with his striking white hair and penchant for black attire, was reputedly chosen for his resemblance to a pint of Guinness. His series of adverts were atmospheric, often surreal and highly philosophical.

He once famously pondered, "It's not easy being a dolphin," a line that encapsulated the campaign's quirky, intellectual depth.

6

From the 1920s to the 1970s, Guinness was given to hospital patients and pregnant or lactating women.

Like red wine and dark chocolate, Guinness contains antioxidants (from the flavonoids in the barley and hops) which can help reduce blood clots and support heart health.

Guinness also contains B vitamins, soluble fibre, and prebiotics, which can aid digestion and gut health. But is Guinness actually good for you?

NOT REALLY.

162,719

The amount of pints of Guinness that go to waste every year due to facial hair.

According to a Guinness-commissioned study from 2000, approximately 0.56 millilitres of stout is trapped in a beard or moustache with every single sip.

6

40 per cent of all Guinness is consumed in Africa, with Nigeria and Cameroon drinking the most.

This makes the continent by far the largest consumer of the stout!

In his early teens, football icon David Beckham was given a unique bulking diet by his father, Ted, ahead of his first trials for Manchester United.

"I was a bit worried about the size of him so that's when we started giving him Guinness and a raw egg. To be fair to the boy, he did it every week."

The diet must have worked, Beckham is now one of the most beloved statesmen for football in the world.

12-18mm

(one half to three quarters of an inch)

The ideal head height on a perfectly poured Guinness.

Anything less, simply isn't Guinness.

“

When things go wrong and will not come right,
Though you do the best you can,
When life looks black as the hour of night –
A pint of plain is your only man.

When money’s tight and hard to get
And your horse has also ran,
When all you have is a heap of debt –
A pint of plain is your only man.

”

FLANN O’BRIEN

The Workman’s Friend, 1940.*

* By 1821, Guinness had perfected its porter recipe. It soon became known in Dublin as “a pint of plain” to differentiate it from stronger stouts. The term also highlighted its status as an affordable drink, favoured by the city’s working class.

“Five-twelfths of an inch is the ideal head around the top, and if somebody paints a shamrock into it, you’re allowed to stab them in the eye with a fork.”

DARA Ó BRIAIN

In December 2025, Guinness opened its first London microbrewery at Old Brewer's Yard in Covent Garden, the first of its kind for Guinness, and the capital city.

The 50,000-square-foot culture hub cost £73 million to build and features a rooftop with 360-degree views, a Guinness merch shop and a micro-brewery pumping out 14 different limited-edition brews.

"I supped at the Carlton, with a large party, of oysters and Guinness, and got to bed at half-past twelve o'clock. Thus ended the most remarkable day hitherto of my life."

BENJAMIN DISRAELI

In December 1837, the future British prime minister wrote this line in his diary after he first tasted the luxurious combination of Guinness and oysters.

Absolute Creamer

Social media sensation Jason Hackett, AKA Prime Mutton, has gained viral fame on YouTube and Instagram for his online reviews of Guinness pints from around UK and Ireland.

He now has more than 200,000 followers. If Jason is impressed with a pint of Guinness, he exclaims his now-iconic catchphrase – "Absolute creamer!"

The best pint of Guinness he's ever had? See page 122.

6

Baby Guinness

While this world-famous shot does not contain Guinness, its appearance mimics a Guinness pint, with its mix of two-parts coffee liqueur to one-part Irish cream.

To make it right, simply pour 30ml of coffee liqueur into a shot glass then, very carefully, slowly pour 15ml of Irish cream liqueur over the back of a spoon held just above the coffee liqueur.

This technique allows the cream to float on top, thus creating the distinctive look of pint of Guinness.

Guinnfluencers

The term coined for social media influencers significantly responsible for bolstering Guinness's popularity among Generation Z (those born between 1997 and 2012).

These digital trendsetters have played a key role in the stout's recent resurgence with younger demographics. Consequently, the largest consumers of Guinness are now predominantly 25 to 35-year-olds, rather than the previously reliable 55 to 64-year-olds.

6

In 2024, Guinness became a viral sensation online for millions of millennials and Generation Z.

The #GuinnessChallenge exploded on Instagram and TikTok with young Guinness drinkers posting their best attempts to split the G.

The popularity of the #GuinnessChallenge was responsible for a 20 per cent surge in demand for Guinness and a UK-wide shortage at Christmas time.

The area around Dublin's St. James's Gate has a profound historical connection to the Camino de Santiago pilgrimage to Spain, one of the world's most popular, drawing over 500,000 pilgrims annually.

For centuries, dating back to medieval times, the Gate was the traditional departure point for Irish pilgrims on route to Santiago de Compostela.

Today, the Guinness Storehouse, situated on the historic site, continues this tradition, offering pilgrims the opportunity to get their Camino passports stamped as they begin their modern-day "Celtic Camino".

September 22, 1955

The day Guinness aired its first ever TV commercial, known as the "Sea Lion". This black and white advert debuted on ITV and was based on the first Gilroy poster advert of a Sea Lion balancing a pint of Guinness on its snout pursued by a zoo keeper.

The advert begins with the line "A Guinness poster comes to life!"

Here's to a long life and
a merry one.

A quick death and an
easy one.

A pretty girl and an
honest one.

A cold pint – and another
one!

6

As of the 2024/2025 season, Guinness is now the Official Beer of the UK's football Premier League, replacing previous brand, Budweiser.

The partnership marks Guinness's first-ever major association with top-tier football.

This now makes Guinness the official beer of both Football and Rugby, as its also the Official Beer of England Rugby and the Six Nations tournament.

346,750,000

The number of pints of Guinness consumed by Americans annually, with a daily consumption of 950,000 pints a day.

This is far behind America's leading beer brand, Modulo Especial, with daily consumption at tens of millions of bottles a day.

6

When it comes to Guinness, two heads are better than one.

St James's Flip

A cocktail that got its name from the home of Guinness, St. James's Gate, the "Flip" is a fresh way to enjoy your favourite stout.

INGREDIENTS

30 ml Black Rum
15 ml sweetened condensed milk
½ fresh egg
44 ml Guinness
Grated nutmeg, to garnish

Combine the rum, milk, egg and Guinness together in a cocktail shaker and shake without ice. Add ice to the shaker and continue to shake until the mixture is smooth and frothy. Strain cocktail into a small goblet and garnish with freshly grated nutmeg. Then make another one.

6

When World War I erupted in 1914, Guinness actively encouraged employees from its St. James's Gate Brewery, Dublin, to join the British forces.

Around 800 staff members served in the conflict.

103 did not return.

Irishman Ian Ryan is the founder of the viral Instagram account, Shit London Guinness, which hilariously documents the capital's worst crimes of badly-poured pints of Guinness and now has more than 250,000 followers on Instagram.

"There's a part of the Irish psyche where you feel downtrodden and you can consider it nearly a sin against your Irish roots to see a bad pint of Guinness," Ryan said as to why he set-up the account.

6

The "Guinness Guru", AKA Darragh Curran, is an Irish social media sensation who rose to fame meticulously reviewing pints of Guinness on TikTok.

Famously, he claimed he has visited almost all of Ireland's 7,000 pubs. In 2023, he travelled to New York to find the best pint of Guinness in Manhattan.

The winner? The Dead Rabbit, an Irish pub, on 30 Water Street, with a score of 7.9 out of 10.

In the 1997 Oscar-winning movie *Good Will Hunting*, the now iconic scene where Skylar (Minnie Driver) tells a "filthy" joke to Will's (Matt Damon) friends in her best Irish accent. The joke's memorable punchline requires Skylar to hold a large gulp of Guinness in her mouth, for reasons about to be made clear...

"All right, there's an old couple in bed, Mary and Paddie. They wake up on the morning of their 50th anniversary. Mary looks over and gazes adoringly at Paddie. She's like, "Oh, Jesus, Paddie. You're such a good-looking feller. I love ya. I want to give ya a little present. Anything your little heart desires, I'm goin' to give it to ya. What would you like?"

6

Paddie's like, "Oh, gee, Mary. That's a very sweet offer. Now, in 50 years, there's one thing that's been missing, and, uh, I would like you to give me a blow job. I would like for it."

Mary's like, "All right." She takes her teeth out, puts 'em in the glass. She gives him a blow job. Afterwards, Paddie's like, "Yeah, geez, now that's what I've been missin'. That was the most beautiful, earth-shattering thing ever! Beautiful, Mary! I love ya! Is there anything that I can do for you?"

Mary looks up to him and she goes, (Skylar takes a swig of her drink) "Give us a kiss."

"

I always thought
Guinness was made of
chunks of peat,
ground up four-leaf clovers,
and whatever you
squeeze out of a
leprechaun to make it
brown.

"

STEPHEN COLBERT

6

"I've only recently gotten into Guinness, which is kind of a sacrilegious thing for an Irish person to say."

PAUL MESCAL

September 15, 1787

The date that 55 of America's Founding Fathers* had the mother of all parties at Philadelphia's City Tavern, following the signing of the U.S. Constitution.

The notorious bar tab included 54 bottles Madeira, 60 bottles Claret, 22 bottles of stout porter*, 12 bottles of beer, 8 bottles of whiskey, 8 bottles of hard ciders, and 7 bowls of punch.

*Several US presidents, notably George Washington and John Adams, were particularly fond of porter.

6

The top 10 countries that drink the most Guinness, in order of volume, are:

Great Britain, Ireland, United States of America, Nigeria, Cameroon, Kenya, Ghana, Jamaica, Indonesia and Malaysia.

"My number one choice is Guinness.
My number two choice would be Guinness.
My number three choice would have to be Guinness."

Peter O'Toole
Actor (1932–2013), when asked, "What's your favourite Irish food?"